D0341033

# SECRETS
## of the CODE

The Unauthorized Guide
to the Mysteries Behind
The Da Vinci Code

*Edited by Dan Burstein*

RUNNING PRESS
PHILADELPHIA • LONDON

Library of Congress Control Number: 2005910394

ISBN-13: 978-0-7624-2852-6
ISBN-10: 0-7624-2852-X

This book may be ordered by mail from the publisher. Please include $1.00 for postage and handling.
*But try your bookstore first!*

Running Press Book Publishers
125 South Twenty-Second Street
Philadelphia, Pennsylvania 19103-4399

Log onto www.specialfavors.com to order Running Press® Miniature Editions™ with your own custom-made covers!

Visit us on the web!
www.runningpress.com

# Contents

# PART III: Keeping the Secrets Secret

# PART IV: Conclusion

# Introduction
*Searching for* Sophia

Like many of you, I came across *The Da Vinci Code* by Dan Brown in the summer of 2003. It was already the number one book on the *New York Times* bestseller list. It sat by my bedside for a while, along with dozens of other unread books, piles of magazines, and business presentations I needed to review. Then one day I picked up *The Da Vinci Code* and started reading. I read all night, fascinated. I literally couldn't put it down.

By morning, I was as intellectually challenged as I had been by any book I had read in a long time. I wanted to know what was true and what was not, what was fact, what was fiction, what was informed speculation and what was pure flight of literary fancy. As soon as my local bookstore opened, I was there rummaging through scores of books that had been mentioned or alluded to in *The Da Vinci Code: Holy Blood, Holy Grail, The Templar Revelation, Gnostic Gospels, The Woman With the Alabaster Jar, The Nag Hammadi Library*, and many more. I left the store with hundreds of dollars' worth of books and went home to absorb all this material. For weeks, I continued to buy books that I discovered were relevant to *The Da Vinci Code*.

As I absorbed all these books and materials and as I continued to talk to friends about their experience of reading *The Da Vinci Code* (DVC), the idea occurred to me that I should try to bring some of these diverse strands together into a single volume, so that other DVC readers and enthusiasts could benefit from the same body of knowledge and criticism that I was exploring. Thus, the idea for this book was born.

Before setting readers off into this volume, I would like to share a variety of observations about why I think *The Da Vinci Code* has struck such a nerve among the reading public and resonates so deeply with the contemporary zeitgeist.

1) DVC is a novel of *ideas*. Say what you will about some of the ham-fisted dialogue and improbable plot elements, Dan Brown has wrapped large complex ideas, as well as minute details and fragments of intriguing thoughts into his action-adventure-murder mystery. Even among much higher-brow, more literary writers, all too few are writing novels that deal with big philosophical, cosmological, or historical concepts. And

among those who are, most of the books they are producing are simply too inaccessible for even the average sophisticated, educated reader. Dan Brown has given us an incredible array of fascinating ideas and concepts.

2) Like James Joyce's *Ulysses*, DVC takes place essentially in one twenty-four-hour period. Like Joyce's *Finnegan's Wake*, it ends where it begins. Clearly, Dan Brown takes literary form quite seriously. He may play faster and looser with facts than some would like, but his ability to compress extensive intellectual and religious argu-

ments into quickly accessible sound bites is an art form.

3) Our materialistic, technological, scientific, information-flooded culture is hungry for a sense of mission and meaning. People are looking for a recovery of their spiritual sensibility, or at least a context for their lives. DVC can be read as a modern *Odyssey* through myth, archetypes, symbolic language, and religious practice. The characters will not only save the most precious secrets from falling into the wrong hands, in the process they will gain knowledge of self, identity, and a place in the world.

4) Like other times in history—the legendary days of Arthur, the Crusades, the nineteenth century—we are living in an era when the romance of the hunt for the Holy Grail is being renewed. This is true in the narrow sense of a huge flourishing of new literature about the Holy Grail of Christian history. Dan Brown draws extensively on this body of occult, New Age, and mysterious work.

5) Women are a large constituency of DVC readers, and the book responds in many ways to new thinking about women in our culture. Dan Brown has rescued Mary Magdalene from the repu-

tation of sin, penitence, and prostitution. I am willing to go out on a limb and guess that far more people may have learned from *The Da Vinci Code* that Mary Magdalene is no longer considered a prostitute than from the official church clarifications of the 1960s. Fourteen hundred years of being seen as a fallen woman is a tough reputation to overcome. But DVC has moved the church's correction off the proverbial page 28 of the third section and on to the front page of the public's consciousness. Not only that. DVC makes the case that Mary Magdalene was much more than "not a prostitute." In the novel's estimation, she was a strong, independent figure, patron of Jesus, cofounder of his movement, his only believer in his greatest hour of need, author of her own Gospel, his romantic partner, and the mother of his child. To the millions of women who feel slighted, discriminated against, or unwelcome in churches of all faiths today, the novel is a chance to see early religious history in an entirely different light. *The Da Vinci Code* opens everyone's eyes to a startlingly different view of the powerful role of women in the birth of Christianity. These themes have become mainstream at Harvard's divinity school and other intellectual centers, but it is DVC that brought this perspective into focus for literate women (and men) who dwell outside academe. The book illuminates how the feminine half of the human equation may have been deliberately suppressed for political reasons by the rise of the institutional, centralized power of the Roman church. Facts presented in DVC—real, verifiable facts—tell a story many people do not know.

6) In a time of growing fundamentalism and religious extremism in the world, DVC offers an important study of Western history. First, it highlights the diversity

and ferment that existed in the Judeo-Christian world two thousand years ago—diversity and ferment that was later suppressed by the antiheresy campaigns of the church. It suggests that some of the pagan and Eastern ideas that found their way into eastern Mediterranean thought may have had value and validity. DVC is an implicit critique of intolerance, of madness in the name of God, and of all those who believe there is only one true God, one true faith, and one true way to practice religious devotion.

7) Tapping into recent archaeological finds—such as the Nag Hammadi texts

and the Dead Sea Scrolls—as well as doing art history analysis of Leonardo and other painters, symbol interpretation, and cryptography, DVC weaves together various strands from the scientific and archaeological reports of our times. In doing so, the novel sketches out elements of the greatest detective story ever told: we are living in an era where we are uncovering authentic evidence about human origins as well as the origins of many ideas and beliefs.

8) The idea that Robert Langdon is a symbologist—an academic pursuit that appears to be Dan Brown's own

coinage—and that Langdon has such a terrific knack for explaining signs and symbols, is another aspect of the book's appeal. In a sense, we are moving backward in time to a period when visual signs and symbols were much more important. The fact that Brown has strewn codes, symbols, and anagrams throughout the book makes it all the more interesting and interactive for us as participants in the experience.

9) Conspiracy, secrecy, privacy, identity theft, technology and its problems—these are themes in all of Dan Brown's books, and they are very appropriate

themes for our time. Reading DVC stimulates thought and discussions on all these subjects. One can't read *The Da Vinci Code* without hearing the echoes of these contemporary incidents of lying and cover-up—and the truth coming out in the end.

Is *The Da Vinci Code* fact or fiction? My primary goal is to give you the materials so you can draw your own conclusion. Let me make it perfectly clear that I do not claim to have great prior expertise on the subjects covered by *The Da Vinci Code*. I have an intense interest and abiding curiosity about these subjects, but no academic, religious, or artistic credentials. I see myself as very much like most of the novel's readers. I became engaged with these ideas and I went out to research them in more depth, find the most well-regarded experts I could to interview, identify the most compelling source material, and bring it all together in a handy single volume designed for other interested, curious readers. My personal conclusion is that the novel is a fascinating, well-crafted work of fiction that is informed throughout by interesting bits of little-known facts and stimulating, but highly speculative thought provocations. It is most valuable when read as a book of ideas and metaphors—a notebook,

Leonardo style, that helps the reader think through his or her own philosophy, cosmology, religious beliefs, or critiques.

The fact that material is presented here doesn't mean I think the arguments presented are true. It only means I think you should hear the arguments and make up your own mind.

What follows in *Secrets of the Code* is a compilation of ideas and opinions from a wide spectrum of thinkers. This book is designed to help the reader on his or her hunt for personal knowledge and insight—sophia, if you will.

Let me be crystal clear: *The Da Vinci Code* is a novel. It is an entertainment. It is something to enjoy. Part of the enjoyment, for me anyway, is to follow upon its threads and ideas, to pursue its interconnections. That's what this book is all about.

—Dan Burstein

# Part I

Mary Magdalene
and the
Sacred Feminine

# 1 MARY MAGDALENE

## How a Woman of Substance Was Harlotized by History

Mary Magdalene is, in many ways, the star of *The Da Vinci Code*, and it is fitting that she should be the starting point for this book's odyssey into exploring the histories and mysteries in Dan Brown's novel. But who was this woman who plays such a key role at critical moments in the traditional Gospels? She is clearly one of the closest companions of the itinerant Jesus. She is among the only followers of Jesus to be present at his crucifixion and she attends to him after his death. She is the person who returns to his tomb three days later and the person to whom the resurrected Jesus first appears. When he appears, he instructs—indeed, he empowers—her to spread the news of his resurrection and to become, in effect, the most important apostle, the bearer of the Christian message to the other apostles and to the world.

All of that is according to state-ments made in the officially accepted

New Testament accounts. If you study the alternative accounts—various lost scriptures and the Gnostic Gospels— you quickly find the hints that Mary Magdalene and Jesus may have had an extremely close relationship, an intimate relationship of man and wife. You find that she may have been a leader and thinker in her own right to whom Jesus may have entrusted secrets that he did not even share with the male apostles. She may have been caught up in a jealous rivalry among the other apostles, some of whom, notably Peter, may have disdained her role in the movement on the basis of her gender and found her relationship with Jesus problematic. She may have represented a more humanistic, individualized philosophy, perhaps closer to that which Jesus actually preached than to what became accepted by the Roman Empire in the time of Constantine as official, standardized, mainstream Christian thinking.

She is perhaps best known in history as a prostitute. But was she ever a prostitute? Did Jesus simply forgive her—and did she simply repent and change her ways—to illustrate traditional Christian principles about sin, forgiveness, penance, and redemption?

Or was she not a prostitute at all, but a wealthy financial patron and supporter of the Jesus movement who was later declared by Pope Gregory in the sixth century to be identical to a different Mary in the Gospels who was, indeed, a prostitute? And when Pope Gregory conflated three different Marys in the Gospels into one, did he do this deliberately to brand Mary Magdalene with the stigma of prostitution? Was it an honest mistake of interpretation in a dark age when few original documents were in hand and biblical language was a mélange of Hebrew, Aramaic, Greek, and Latin? Did the church need to simplify and codify the Gospels and to play up the themes of sin, penance and redemption? Or was it a far more Machiavellian stratagem (a millennium before Machiavelli) to ruin Mary Magdalene's reputation in history and, by doing so, destroy the last vestiges of the influences of pagan goddess cults and the "sacred feminine" on early Christianity, to undermine the role of women in the church and bury the more humanistic side of Christian faith?

Did it go even further? When Pope Gregory placed the scarlet letter of prostitution on Mary Magdalene—who would remain officially a reformed prostitute for the next fourteen centuries—was it the beginning of the great cover-up to deny the marriage of Jesus and Mary Magdalene and, ultimately, the royal, sacred bloodline of their offspring?

Their offspring? Well, yes. If Jesus and Mary Magdalene were married or at least had an intimate relationship, there might well have been a child or children. And what did happen to Mary Magdalene after the crucifixion? The Bible is silent, but around the Mediterranean, from Ephesus to Egypt, there is legend and lore suggesting Mary Magdalene, with her child (or children), escaped from Jerusalem and eventually settled down to the life of an evangelist. The most interesting stories have her living out her years in France . . . a theme Dan Brown picks up and makes integral to the plot of *The Da Vinci Code*.

Representing issues about sin and redemption, the Madonna and the whore, penitence and virtue, the faithful and the fallen, it is no surprise that Mary Magdalene has always been a towering figure in literature and culture.

In much more recent times, Dan Brown is not the first author to be fascinated with Mary Magdalene, nor the first to play up the issue of her possible marriage to Jesus. Nikos Kazantzakis posited a romantic relationship between them in his novel *The Last Temptation of Christ* more than fifty years ago (well before Martin Scorsese turned it into a movie in the 1980s and raised the issue again). William E. Phipps addressed many of these same issues in his book *Was Jesus Married?*, more than thirty years ago. The rock opera *Jesus Christ Superstar*, another work that hails from more than thirty years ago, also assumes a romantic relationship between Jesus and Mary Magdalene. Given our society's interest in issues about gender roles, women as leaders, and all the permutations of love, marriage, and sex, one can imagine, the "new" Mary Magdalene fits right in, and *The Da Vinci Code* is right on time.

In this chapter, we include an interview with Susan Haskins, an expert on Mary Magdalene and the author of the book *Mary Magdalen: Myth and Metaphor*. Susan discusses who she thinks Mary Magdalene was, why she may have been misrepresented, and what may have been the relationship between Mary Magdalene and Jesus.

Dan Brown has done quite a job in

*The Da Vinci Code* of alluding to many of the mysteries surrounding Mary Magdalene. In a handful of pages, in the midst of a murder mystery-thriller-detective story, he manages to refer to the many ambiguities shrouding this biblical figure... most notably the possibility that Leonardo da Vinci knew and understood the real history of Jesus Christ and Mary Magdalene and that's why he painted Mary Magdalene into *The Last Supper*. Moreover, the image of a leering Peter, slicing his bladelike hand in Mary Magdalene's direction in the painting, is meant, according to *The Da Vinci Code*, to suggest the animosity between Peter and Mary Magdalene over the future of the church. In the novel, Sophie Neveu asks her late-night teachers, Teabing and Langdon, "You're saying the Christian Church was to be carried on by a woman?"

"That was the plan," says Teabing. "Jesus was the original feminist. He intended for the future of His Church to be in the hands of Mary Magdalene."

One can see why the issues of *The Da Vinci Code* have people talking, arguing, searching—however improbable some aspects of the plot may be and however rewoven or spun out of whole cloth the religious history may be. Authorities like Susan Haskins (and many others) are well-credentialed academics who have spent years studying the most arcane details from the available information about Mary Magdalene and related issues. They all believe that she has been mistreated in history. They eschew the most extreme ideas about her, but are consciously working to create a new multifaceted, nuanced view of Mary Magdalene restored to her rightful place in history.

# Mary Magdalene
*The Model for Women
in the Church*

## AN INTERVIEW
## WITH SUSAN HASKINS

Susan Haskins is the author of *Mary Magdalen:
Myth and Metaphor.*

*In your opinion, who was the true Mary
Magdalene?*

The true Mary Magdalene is the figure in the Gospels: the leading woman
follower of Christ, who, together with the
other women named in Luke, supported
and contributed to the living expenses of

the itinerant group. She was present at his crucifixion, witnessed it, and according to John's Gospel, was one of the privileged few, along with the Virgin Mary, wife of Cleophas, and St. John, to be beneath the cross. She was witness to the putting of his body in Joseph of Arimathea's sepulcher; she came at dawn with either one or two other Marys to bring unguents. In John's Gospel, it was to her alone and first that Christ appeared after his resurrection, and it was to her alone and first that he gave the message of the new Christian life. Mark's Gospel, in a later addition, says that she had had seven devils driven from her. We have no idea of what she looked like. She is shown with long red or golden hair in medieval and later art, because blond hair was the attribute of ideal feminine beauty. We do not know what her life was like. It is assumed that because she, along with the other women followers, supported the group "of their own substance," that she was mature—among the other women were ones who were married or separated—and comparatively well off and independent. So I agree with those who see her as a patron and supporter of Jesus.

*What are the representations of Mary Magdalene that have occurred through-*

*out history? Do any of them fit with Dan Brown's theory in* The Da Vinci Code *that she may have been married to Jesus and had his child?*

Dan Brown's theory that Mary Magdalene may have been married to Jesus and had his child has a long history. It was made particularly public by *Holy Blood, Holy Grail*, and followed up by Bishop Spong and others. Luther seems to have thought that she had a sexual relationship with Christ as far back as the sixteenth century! As there is no concrete evidence of either a marriage or child, I would give no credence to this hypothesis.

*Why did the church depict Mary Magdalene as a prostitute for so many years? Was she simply a victim of bad luck to be confused with all of the other Marys in the New Testament, or was there a kind of foul play involved?*

The church depicted Mary Magdalene as a prostitute because of the various commentaries on the Gospels made by early church fathers from the third century, trying to work out who all the Gospel characters were. There are several females called Mary in the New Testament, which led to confusion. Because Luke's first mention of Mary Magdalene, following Christ from

Galilee with the other women, and the male disciples follows his account of the unnamed woman named as a sinner, forgiven by Christ in the house of the Pharisee, Pope Gregory the Great (A.D. 595) conflated these two figures, as well as that of Mary of Bethany. Although the woman is only called a "sinner," the assumption was that her sin was that of the flesh, even though the word *porin*, used to describe her, does not mean "prostitute." Making Mary Magdalene a repentant prostitute diminished her role as first apostle, an otherwise extremely powerful and important role. We cannot know for sure whether foul play was involved, but certainly ecclesiastical politics were. The early church had women priests and bishops, but by the fifth century the sacerdotal role was not allowed to women, although tomb monuments in southern Italy show that women were still carrying out the priestly role. Diminishing Mary Magdalene's role to both penitent and prostitute puts her on a par with Eve, whose sexuality and gender were deemed by the male ecclesiastical hierarchy as being responsible for the Fall.

*Do you think that Jesus and Mary Magdalene could have been married?*

I personally do not think Jesus and Mary Magdalene were married. That an important relationship existed between them is undeniable, but was it any more than the fact that she was his leading woman disciple? People find the idea compelling for many reasons: there is this enigmatic relationship in the Gospels— even more so in the Gnostic Gospels—so a kind of logical progression would be marriage. Rabbis were often, if not usually, married, so it has often been suggested that Christ must also have been, although there is nothing in the Gospels to suggest this. We have no evidence of a child, and the Merovingian link is very unlikely.

*How does* The Da Vinci Code *character of Mary Magdalene fit in with other characters in prior religious belief systems? Is there a woman comparable to Mary Magdalene in Greek, Egyptian, Jewish, or pagan/tribal cultures?*

The Da Vinci Code is interesting for its narrative re: the goddess figure, suppressed by the early church. The theme of resurrection is found in Egyptian, Sumerian, and Christian belief systems: Isis and Osiris, Ishtar and Tammuz, Mary Magdalene and Christ. Mary Magdalene can be seen as the Christian goddess.

*Why was Mary Magdalene one of the few at the crucifixion? Why might she have attended when other disciples did not? And what is the importance of Mary Magdalene being the first to see Jesus after the resurrection?*

It is interesting that Mary Magdalene was one of the few at the crucifixion. But this is only in John's account; in the others, she witnesses it from a distance, with other women. We do not know who edited the Gospel texts or why they are only approximately identical, but presumably they come from different oral traditions. The women disciples were there, but not the males because the males had taken fright, particularly Peter, who denied Jesus thrice.

It is, or should be, of the utmost importance to Christians that it was to Mary Magdalene that Jesus appeared first after the resurrection, because the keystone to Christianity is the promise of everlasting life—the very message Christ gave to her to tell the world. It was male prejudice in both the Judaic and Hellenistic systems that disallowed women as witnesses and therefore allowed the male disciples to claim the right to give the news of the resurrection. But, of course, it can be seen as equally important—as a matter of editing the

canon, Christian apologetics, and ecclesiastical politics—for the church to deny
this role and to assert the premise that
"You are Peter and upon this rock I will
found my church."

# 2 THE SACRED FEMININE

*The sacred feminine is that other face of God that has not been honored over the two millennia of Christianity—at least not as a fully equal partner.*—Margaret Starbird

In this chapter, we explore the background to the "sacred feminine" thesis that lies at the heart of *The Da Vinci Code*'s plot. As readers of the novel will recall, almost on arrival in the middle of the night at Leigh Teabing's Château

Villette, Sophie Neveu finds herself immersed in explanations and theoretical pyrotechnics from Teabing and Langdon about the Holy Grail, Mary Magdalene, and the sacred feminine. Langdon tells Sophie: "The Holy Grail represents the sacred feminine and the goddess . . . The power of the female and her ability to produce life was once very sacred, but it posed a threat to the rise of the predominantly male Church, and so the sacred feminine was demonized and called unclean . . . When Christianity came along, the old pagan religions did not die easily. Legends of chivalric quests for the lost Grail were in fact stories of forbidden quests to find the lost sacred feminine. Knights who claimed to be 'searching for the chalice' were speaking in code as a way to protect themselves from a Church that had subjugated women, banished the Goddess, burned nonbelievers, and forbidden the pagan reverence for the sacred feminine."

The case for the sacred feminine—suppressed goddess—Mary Magdalene analysis that Langdon and Teabing lay out for Sophie raises some of the most intellectually fascinating questions in the novel. To be sure, it is implausible in many respects, especially the way this set of mysteries has been wrapped into the enigmas of the plot. But it is profoundly interesting. In making his late-night case, the fictional Langdon draws heavily on several of the experts, including: Margaret Starbird, Elaine Pagels, Timothy Freke and Peter Gandy, Riane Eisler, and others.

In the following interview, one of these experts, Timothy Freke, puts forward his own argument about the role of the sacred feminine in the development of Western culture, thought, politics, philosophy, and religion.

# The Godman
# and the Goddess

## AN INTERVIEW
## WITH TIMOTHY FREKE

Timothy Freke has a degree in philosophy. Peter
Gandy has an M.A. in classical civilizations,
specializing in ancient pagan mystery religions.
They are the coauthors of *Jesus and the Lost
Goddess: The Secret Teachings of the Original
Christians*, as well as *The Jesus Mysteries: Was
the "Original Jesus" a Pagan God*? and more
than twenty other books.

In this interview, Freke introduces some of the argument in *Jesus and the Lost Goddess*. Freke and Gandy are key architects of the argument that holds that the belief system of the original Christians was thoroughly subverted as the Roman Empire institutionalized Christianity. The early Christian movement's beliefs in the Gnostic experience of mystical enlightenment and the mystical union of the Godman (Jesus) and the Goddess (Mary Magdalene) were so threatening to the Roman church's vision that they had to be brutally suppressed. The Goddess as well as the mystical and Gnostic traditions, was then written out of the documents, beliefs, and practices of Christianity. For the original Christians, as Teabing tells Sophie in *The Da Vinci Code* about the Priory of Sion's efforts to keep alive the Goddess tradition, Mary Magdalene represents "the Goddess, the Holy Grail, the Rose, and the Divine Mother."

*What was the importance of Goddess worship in pagan cultures?*

Along with the myth of the Godman, the pagan mysteries told an allegorical myth of the lost and redeemed Goddess, that was an allegory about the fall and redemption of the soul. The most famous pagan version of this myth is Demeter and Persephone. The original Christians adapted this into their myth of Sophia—the Christian Goddess whose name means "wisdom."

*What is distinctly "feminine" about Sophia?*

The Goddess represents the All, the universe, all that we sense, all that we imagine—the flow of appearances, forms, experience. God—the male archetype—represents the One, the mysterious source of all consciousness which conceives and witnesses the flow of appearances we call life. (Life, or Zoë, was another name of the Christian Goddess). Sophia was already being venerated by Jewish and pagan mystics before the rise of Christianity.

*But the Goddess is not always portrayed in only one light.*

Christian mythology is deep and multilayered. This relationship plays out in many ways on many levels. From the arising of something from nothing, it eventually becomes the relationship between Jesus and the two Marys who represent the two aspects of the Goddess—virgin mother and fallen and redeemed whore. Again, these are images taken from ancient pagan mythology.

*How does Eve fit into the "lost Goddess" tradition?*

She represents half (not a rib as is often mistranslated) of Adam (whose name means "human"). Her myth mirrors pagan myths of the fall of the soul into incarnation, which the Jesus myth seeks to redress.

*What is the philosophical concept behind the sacred feminine?*

The male principle for the ancients was indivisible consciousness. The female principle was the multitude of appearances, experiences, what is being witnessed. This duality is fundamental to life. Without it there is nothing. Wisdom is the state of the soul (feminine principle) when it is pure enough to recognize its true nature, to be the One Consciousness in all, which was symbolized for Paul and company by the Christ or "King."

# Part II

Echoes
of the
Hidden Past

# 3 THE LOST GOSPELS

The religious girders that frame the edifice of Dan Brown's plot are built upon the foundations of early Christian history and, in particular, the set of Gnostic Gospels found in 1945 near the Egyptian town of Nag Hammadi. These documents, which have led to remarkable discoveries about an alternate tradition later suppressed, form the backdrop of another artful blending of fact and fiction in *The Da Vinci Code*. In Chapter

58, which takes place in Lee Teabing's sumptuous study, Sophie Neveu and Robert Langdon are handed a copy of these lost Gospels in a "leather-bound . . . poster-sized" edition to demonstrate with irrevocable proof that "the marriage of Jesus and Mary Magdalene is part of the historical record."

There is no doubt the Nag Hammadi texts have yielded a treasure trove of documents permitting a richer, more nuanced and, perhaps, even more radical interpretation of the words of Jesus, the role of his followers, and the interpretation of early Christianity. They help shed light on a time when the many contending schools of Christian worship were interwoven and the definitive canon had not yet been created. Specifically, they give our era a glimpse into a different tradition—the Gnostic Tradition—that conflicted with the interpretation of Jesus' preaching found today in the orthodoxy of the New Testament. More explosively, in terms of the history of the church, they suggest a much more important role for Mary Magdalene as a disciple and close companion to Jesus. They also suggest more interest in seeking inner knowledge and self-development than what we traditionally understand as the philosophy of the New Testament. And the Gnostics of Nag Hammadi seemed to feel less need for churches and priests. They seemed perfectly comfortable interpreting their own Gospels and sacred books without intermediation— an idea institutionalized Christianity would find threatening.

In the following interview, we invite readers to join in the search for the meaning and implications of these lost Gospels. Certainly they seem to emphasize a balance between the masculine and the feminine, the good and the evil in mankind, and the importance of Mary Magdalene as an apostle.

# What the Nag Hammadi Texts Tell Us about "Liberated" Christianity

## AN INTERVIEW WITH JAMES M. ROBINSON

James Robinson is Professor of Religion Emeritus, Claremont Graduate University, and general editor, The Nag Hammadi Library. He is one of the world's leading authorities on early Christianity and supervised the team of scholars and translators who brought the lost Gospels to life.

*As one of the leading scholars of what we know as the lost Gospels, what is your reaction to seeing these historic*

*ideas suddenly being propelled onto the
bestseller list with the popularity of* The
Da Vinci Code?

The book has had a sensationalist
kind of success, which worries scholars
such as myself who are trying to stick
to the facts. I think there is a certain
built-in problem of this book being a
novel, and therefore saying it's fiction
but, at the same time, using enough
facts, well-known names and things
like the Nag Hammadi discovery to
give it a semblance of factual accuracy.
It is hard for the lay public to distin-
guish where one begins and the other
leaves off. So, strictly from that point of

view, it's very misleading.

Moreover, it is clear to me that Dan Brown doesn't know much about the scholarly side of things in my field and he sort of fudges the evidence to make it more sensational than it is. As an example, he refers to the Nag Hammadi find as "scrolls," but they are not. They are codexes—books with individual pages. Indeed, it is actually the oldest example we have of leather-bound books. Elsewhere, Dan Brown refers to the *Gospel Q*, writing, "Allegedly it is a book of Jesus' teach-ings, possibly written with His own hand." What is interesting is that while

it is mentioned, it is not discussed—
perhaps because it would not help his
argument since we know Jesus didn't
write it. These are just some of the
ideas thrown into the novel that are
more sensational than factual.

*So how would you characterize the Nag
Hammadi texts?*

The canonical Gospels, Matthew,
Mark, Luke, and John are a sort of theological biography of Jesus. By con-
trast, the Nag Hammadi Gospels are
not Gospels in the traditional use of
that word to mean narrative history, but
what we now call a sayings Gospel.

The *Gospel of Philip*, for example, is a scattering of materials that is not an original document, but some sort of collection of excerpts from various sources. The *Gospel of Truth* is a quasi-philosophical theological treatise, but it doesn't tell the story of Jesus in any sense of the word. The only one that can claim in some sense to be what we might call a Gospel is the fourth Nag Hammadi text (the *Gospel of Thomas*), which uses the word *Gospel* as a secondary title appended at the end. The opening of the text, however, calls it "secret sayings." It's a collection of sayings, like the sayings behind Matthew and Luke, which is called theoretically Q, and which is mentioned once in *The Da Vinci Code*.

*Do we know anything about the people who might have written these texts?*

They were most likely written by different people at different times. If they were written in the second and third centuries, the authors would likely have been Gnostics, part of a Gnostic movement that was almost competing with emerging orthodox Christianity for who had the right form of Christianity. The orthodox movement had books called Gospels that are known as Mathew,

Mark, Luke, and John. The Gnostic side attached the word Gospel to some of their tracts, which really weren't Gospels, like those in the New Testament, since the canonical Gospels are narratives that speak to the theological biography of Jesus. The Nag Hammadi Gospels are more like a collection of scattered excerpts.

*Would you flesh out this idea of competing Christianities?*

The writers of these codices were attempting to influence what we might call left-wing Christianity—somewhat similar to the New Age phenomenon in our time. They thought that the dominant church of the day (in *The Da Vinci Code* called the Roman Catholic Church) was too earth bound, too worldly, too materialistic, too physical and had missed the spiritual, allegorical, higher, heavenly secret meaning of all of this. And that's what they were supporting.

*Talking about New Age, does the word companion in the* Gospel of Philip *imply for you, as it does for some students of these documents, that Jesus and Mary were married? And even that they kissed?*

No, it doesn't automatically mean married or unmarried. Companion is not necessarily a sex-related term as it might be construed in our day and age. It seems to me it might have been simply a way to pump up the story, to make it more intriguing. If one reads the entire *Gospel of Philip* it becomes clear that the writer disdains physical sex as beastly, literally comparing it to animals. In the early church, a kiss was known as a metaphor for giving birth. And too much has been made out of this kiss. It was also called the Kiss of Peace, somewhat analogous to a modern church service where they ask you to shake hands with everybody and say, "May the peace of Christ be with you."

Regarding designating Mary Magdalene as Jesus' companion, Brown says Aramaic scholars know this means wife. But the *Gospel of Philip* is in Coptic, translated from Greek, so there is no word in the text for Aramaic scholars to consider.

I think the only relevant text for historical information about Mary Magdalene is the New Testament, and it does not go beyond saying that she was one of the circle of women who accompanied the wandering Jesus and his male followers. I think the seven demons that Jesus cast out of her may have referred to some sort of nervous problem or mental illness, like epilepsy. She was challenged, he helped her, and she became a disciple, loyal to the bitter end. I also think she was alone after the execution because the other disciples were cowards. They were likely to have been arrested. The Romans felt women were not important enough to arrest, so they let Mary grieve, figuring she would soon enough melt into the crowds. No doubt the New Testament gives an accurate protrayal of all of these Marys having been there at the time of the crucifixion and on Easter Sunday, to the extent that one gives historical credence to any of the empty-tomb stories.

# 4 THE EARLY DAYS OF CHRISTIANITIES

*One form of Christianity . . . emerged as victorious from the conflicts of the second and third centuries. This one form of Christianity decided what was the "correct" Christian perspective; it decided who could exercise authority over Christian belief and practice; and it determined what forms of Christianity would be marginalized, set aside, destroyed. It also decided which books to canonize into Scripture and which books to set aside as "heretical," teaching false ideas . . .*

*Only twenty-seven of the early Christian books were finally included in the canon, copied by scribes through the ages, eventually translated into English, and now on bookshelves in virtually every home in America. Other books came to be rejected, scorned, maligned, attacked, burned, all but forgotten—lost.*—Bart D. Ehrman

In the beginning, there was not one Christianity, but many. And among them was a well-established tradition of Gnosticism, one of the key "heresies" upon which Dan Brown builds the plot of *The Da Vinci Code*.

Sacred roots and twenty centuries of primacy in the Western world have led to the generally dominant view that modern Christianity evolved more or less linearly and directly from the teachings of Jesus. The snapshot Western civilization has tended to see is a natural progression: starting with Jesus and followed by the preaching of the apostles as depicted in the New Testament, on through the establishment of the church by Peter, brought under the wing of Constantine and the Council of Nicea, and from thence throughout the Roman Empire, Europe, and on into the modern world.

Dan Brown's *The Da Vinci Code* wants to acquaint the reader with the lesser known, even "hidden" side of the story, the unanswered questions about the early history of Christianity.

Early Christian history proceeds to an untidy story punctuated by loose ends, unknowns, intrigues both political and personal, ironies, and considerable doses of what in today's political vernacular might be called "spin." As it turns out, the history of Christianity is primarily one of widely and sometimes wildly differing understandings of what correct Christian belief is, and considerable zeal in the identification and persecution of those thought not to believe correctly.

Scholars have long known that there is roughly a forty-year gap (maybe less, but maybe much more) between the death of Jesus and the writing of the first Gospel. During that period the followers of Jesus were consolidating their beliefs through oral tradition, and deciding who Jesus was and what his life and death meant. Each Gospel was an evangelist's telling of the story from a somewhat different point of view, based on the teller's own circumstances and audience. Eventually, four Gospels and twenty-three other texts were canonized (declared to be the Holy Scriptures) into a Bible. This did not occur, however, until the sixth century.

As Deirdre Good points out in her lectures on Mary Magdalene and *The Da Vinci Code*, "Virtually everyone in the New Testament should be thought of as Jewish unless you can produce any evidence to suggest they are not." Most experts agree that Jesus was a Jew.

Indeed, there was so much ferment in Judaism in those days—different cults, sects, clans, tribes, prophets, false prophets, rabbis, teachers, the Greek-influenced, the Roman-influenced—that the Jesus movement may not have appeared as anything shockingly new or different when it first emerged. The Jewish communities scattered across Egypt, Turkey, Greece, Syria, Iraq, and elsewhere all had their own traditions of modified beliefs and influences drawn from their surrounding cultures. Judaism in those days was a big tent—even if under it, things were often unruly, fractious, and bitterly—even fatally—divided.

It would certainly appear that for a long time after the death of Jesus, his followers were not necessarily perceived as believers in a fundamentally different religion. What became Christianity was initially Jews preaching an increasingly different form of Judaism to other Jews.

Sometimes called Nazareans by Jews and Christians by gentiles (non-Jews), some of the circles of Jesus' followers required that males be circumcised and that the Jewish ritual and dietary laws be followed, yet they professed belief that Jesus was the Son of God and the sole path to salvation—beliefs inconsistent with Jewish orthodoxy. Ebionites, described recently as "Christians still climbing out of their Jewish shell," insisted that to be part of their movement one had to be Jewish. Yet, as Bart Ehrman, the contemporary expert on lost Christian beliefs and scriptures argues, the Ebionites believed deeply in Jesus, but they saw him as "the Jewish Messiah sent from the Jewish God to the Jewish people in fulfillment of the Jewish scripture." The Ebionites believed that Jesus was a mortal man who was so righteous that God adopted him as His son and allowed his sacrifice to redeem humanity's sins.

The apostles, and later their followers, went forth to spread the "good news." The spread of Christianity was a protracted, complicated, and decidedly messy process, that must be viewed within the context of the political world in the early centuries of this era. This was the time of the Roman Empire. As the Empire spread geographically, it incorporated populations whose religious beliefs were primarily pagan and naturalistic, tied to Greek and Egyptian mythology. These existed side by side, with the state taking no side.

It was within this theological stew that Christianity arose. Against the dominant polytheistic religions, Christianity and Judaism were monotheistic, teaching an entirely different relationship of man to God (as opposed to man to gods), and a decidedly different path to salvation. Along the way, many diverse interpretations of the Christian belief system arose, some borrowing elements from the surrounding pagan traditions and others simply having alternate interpretations of key doctrinal beliefs.

Against all the commotion of this backdrop, yet another trend to emerge—and one especially relevant to those interested in the real background of *The Da Vinci Code*'s version of history—was Gnosticism. Gnostics sought knowledge in a mystical, cosmological, and secret sense. They tended to fuse Christianity as a philosophy with more Greek, Egyptian, mythic, and even Eastern elements. Gnostics seem to have been highly literate and to have inherited a mix of the Greek and rabbinic traditions of forming schools to share knowledge and discussion. Bearing in mind that in this time period religion, science, philosophy, politics, poetry, cosmology, and mysticism were all essentially flowing into one primordial soup, the Gnostics created a rich variety of documents, scriptures, and gospels. Representing a variant of Christianity at sharp odds with the increasingly dominant Pauline Christians, the Gnostics were declared to be heretics to be opposed and suppressed.

Over the first two centuries, Christianity morphed from belief taught by itinerant evangelists to small communities of believers organized in local churches—each with its own leaders, writings, and beliefs—with no overarching authority or hierarchy. Slowly at first, then with increasing rapidity, a formal hierarchy came about, and with it a need for doctrinal uniformity. Bishops met in synods to declare what was doctrinally correct. Other views were heresies to be eradicated.

In 313 Emperor Constantine declared that it was "salutary and most proper" that "complete toleration" should be given by the Roman Empire to anyone who had "given up his mind either to the cult of the Christians" or any other similar cult. With this Edict of Milan, official persecution of Christianity and Christians was supposed to end. It is often said that Constantine converted to Christianity, but most scholars understand that this was not until much later, near his death. Many historians believe Constantine's decision can best be explained as politically astute—a move that took into account the accumulating power of Christianity, and a way to put that power at his disposal. Moreover, it was a decision born of a fascinating mix of mystical, superstitious, military, and philosophical threads, in addition to the political impetus. As the historian Paul Johnson notes, Constantine was a "sun-worshipper, one of a number of late-pagan cults which had observances in common with Christians. Thus, the followers of Isis adored a Madonna nursing her holy child," and the followers of Mithras, many of whom were senior military men, celebrated their deity in much the same way Christians would celebrate Christ. "Constantine was almost certainly a Mithraic . . . Many Christians did not make a clear distinction between this sun cult and their own. They referred to Christ driving his chariot across the sky" and held a feast on December 25, considered the sun's birthday at winter solstice. Whatever the reality, this was a major turning point in

Christian history. When the state became at least nominally Christian, the presiding bishops became judicial and administrative as well as scriptural authorities. Constantine and the church both gained power.

A major thorn in Constantine's side was the ongoing controversy with the followers of Arius (Arians) who disputed the notion that Jesus was of the same substance as the Father. Only the Father was God, said Arius and his followers; Christ was not a deity. Constantine wanted the matter settled, and so in 325 convened the Council of Nicea, which declared Arianism a heresy. Heresies from the early church point of view had always been struggled against, and would continue to be—from the Sabellian heresy which said that the Father and the Son were different aspects of one Being rather than distinct persons, to the Inquisition and the Salem witch trials. Although the various shades of opinion of Arians and Donatists and other heretical groups are foggy to us today, the historical record is quite clear that Constantine stepped in and personally presided over the Council of Nicea, even crafting some of the language that came out of the meeting as the ultimate statement on the controversies. What did and didn't happen at the Council of Nicea is a subject of debate between Dan Brown in *The Da Vinci Code* and what many religious practitioners and scholars believe. But Dan Brown's version is highly compelling in this key sense: this was a power struggle over the intellectual infrastructure that would rule much of European politics and thought for the following thousand years. Nicea was not about truth or veracity of religious or moral vision. Ruling some ideas in and others out was fundamentally about politics and power. From Constantine at Nicea to Pope Gregory nearly three hundred years later (and much in between) turns out, at least in retrospect, to have been all about developing the intellectual and political infrastructure of Europe for the next thousand years. You might say it was about codification of the code.

# 5 CONSOLIDATION OR COVER-UP?

## The Establishment of the One True Faith

The metaphorical junction of Christian theology and the struggle for control of the church presented itself as a series of forks in the road during the first five or six hundred years after the death of Christ. Where these roads led, how they clashed, and what the overt and covert meaning of the outcome was, is the subject matter for this chapter.

To achieve primacy, the early church fathers believed they needed to turn Christianity into a force to unite and strengthen the empire. Those who led the Roman Empire in this pursuit believed that a key task was to distill a core ideology and cosmology out of all the various ideas that made up the Christian message. In doing so, they chose to glorify certain Gospel accounts that reinforced their version of Christendom's message—even to select those to be included in the Bible and in what order—at the same time as they vigorously rejected as heretical anything seen as politically or textually deviating from the mainstream.

The Gnostics—far from the centers in Rome and Constantinople—ended up on the defensive in this battle. As Timothy Freke and Peter Gandy argue, the church was systematically eliminating Gnostic and other "heretical" influences, even those that may have been closer to the beliefs and practices of the original revolution Jesus had started, in favor of those that served the cause of consolidating a standardized, hierarchical, powerful church. Down one path lay mystics having ecstatic experiences in the desert; down the other lay strong popes, central cathedrals, and motivated

Christian soldiers prepared to march forward.

Bart Ehrman, an authority on the early church and the life of Jesus, as well as chair of the Department of Religious Studies at the University of North Carolina at Chapel Hill, states "Once Constantine converts to Christianity, he converts to an orthodox form of Christianity, and once the state has power, and the state is Christian, then the state starts asserting its influence over Christianity. So by the end of the fourth century, there's actually legislation against heretics. So the empire that used to be completely anti-Christian becomes

Christian, and not just becomes Christian, but tries to dictate what shape Christianity ought to be."

Some of the most influential writers of the second and third centuries, Tertullian, Irenaeus, and Eusebius, were real, historically well-documented figures of the early church. They played a critical, if sometimes inadvertent, role in selecting which Gospels and which texts would become the New Testament and the modern Christian canon, as well as in destroying—intellectually, ideologically, and physically—the "heretical" Christian movements of those days. Although their names are scarcely known today to the average person of Christian faith, they wielded extraordinary power over determining the ultimate content of modern Christianity. They were the editors, so to speak, of the Bible. Reacting as they were to the severe repression of Christians they had witnessed, these church leaders developed their own biases, and have to be understood in their own context.

With the benefit of more than sixteen hundred years of hindsight, some experts now see those Gnostic "heretics" denounced by early church officialdom as having been on a more humanist, more meaningful, more feminist, and more "Christian" spiritual path than those who ultimately triumphed. If ever there were a case of the winners getting to write history the way they saw it, this is it. Out of this epoch-defining process came a small number of Gospel truths on one side, and a great many heretical documents on the other.

# 6 SECRET SOCIETIES

Like a good spy thriller, the plot of *The Da Vinci Code* moves from one stunning secret to another, from one coded message to the next, from an ancient conspiracy to a modern one, exploring all the while some of the most fundamental secrets of the archaic past of human culture and even archaic areas of the brain itself where primal myths and Jungian archetypes cavort and secret fears, compulsions, and ancient traumas reside.

Dan Brown has said that Robert Ludlum is among his favorite writers, and you can see in *The Da Vinci Code* a touch of vintage Ludlum: start with incredibly compelling and powerful secrets, throw an ordinary man (and a beautiful woman) into fast-paced, high-stakes action to figure out these secrets against the ticking clock of a threat to civilization, confront the characters with deep, dark, powerful secret societies no one thought still existed, bend their minds around conspiracies so intricate the reader can't ever really diagram the plot, and wrap it all into action fast-paced enough to make the reader forget the cardboard characters and the plot holes. The role of secret societies in such plots is not to be understated.

In this chapter, we look especially at two of the most talked about in *The Da Vinci Code*: the Knights Templar and the Priory of Sion.

As *The Da Vinci Code* points out, everyone loves a good conspiracy. Everyone finds it interesting to be let in on a mind-boggling secret. In the case of the two most prominent secret societies in *The Da Vinci Code*—the Templars and the Priory—each one is a fascinating world unto itself. The novel compresses the essence of these secret cultures into some easy-to-understand background material. But then it goes on to exaggerate greatly each one's power, influence, and history.

The Templars, for example, may have had some cultlike practices in medieval days that could be construed as sacred sex rites. Mary Magdalene may have figured more prominently in their culture than in contemporaneous Christianity. And they may well have found treasure in Jerusalem and built a nexus of power and influence. But it is extremely doubtful that they cared much for the theory of the sacred feminine or that they believed the Holy Grail had anything to do with Mary Magdalene's womb and the royal bloodline of the offspring she may or may not have had.

The Priory of Sion, while interesting to speculate about, may never have really existed as anything more than a minor political arm of the Templars during their heyday. As for the modern era, the idea of the Priory may be a complete canard in its twentieth-century incarnation. Leonardo da Vinci may well have been involved with secret sects, heretical philosophies, and unusual sexual practices—and his paintings may well have sought to pass on secret knowledge (or at least make insider jokes) to future generations. But it is highly unlikely Leonardo served as a "grand master" of a functioning secret organization, while leaving not a single clue or bit of documentary evidence behind amid the tens of thousands of pages of notebooks he left to posterity. The same could be said about the other alleged grand masters. With all we know about the lives of Victor Hugo and Jean Cocteau, Newton and Debussy, don't you think there would be a scrap of corroborating evidence somewhere? And for an organization that is supposed to hold the sacred feminine in such high esteem (at least according to the novel), how come there are no prominent women on the list?

Dan Brown, like many novelists, exaggerates even to extremes and lets his imagination run wild for the express purpose of creating the right metaphors and the right thought provocations to rise above the clutter in this information and entertainment saturated world. His approach has had demonstrable success. He got our attention for secret societies and esoteric knowledge, which we had heard of, vaguely, but knew little about. Welcome to the nether world of *The Da Vinci Code*'s secret societies.

# Researching Western Civilization's Darkest Secrets

## AN INTERVIEW WITH LYNN PICKNETT AND CLIVE PRINCE

Lynn Picknett and Clive Prince are London-based writers, researchers, and lecturers on the paranormal, the occult, and historical and religious mysteries. Their book, *The Templar Revelation*, is one of the key books in *The Da Vinci Code*'s bibliography and the original source of a number of the novel's theories about Leonardo, the Templars, and the Priory of Sion. For our book, we interviewed the two of them by email, to follow-up on some of the questions we thought readers might have after reading their material. Excerpts from the interview follow.

*What are the Dossiers Secrets that are
in the Bibliothèque Nationale in Paris,
and why does Dan Brown give them
such prominence in* The Da Vinci Code?

*Dossiers Secrets* is a convenient
term, coined by Baigent, Leigh, and
Lincoln in *Holy Blood, Holy Grail*, for a
set of seven related documents of vary-
ing lengths—in total, less than fifty
pages—deposited in the library between
1964 and 1967.

They deal with subjects such as the
Priory of Sion, the Rennes-le-Château
mystery, Mary Magdalene, and the
Merovingians. The purpose of the documents is to establish the existence of the

Priory of Sion and its role as guardian of historical and esoteric secrets, but *Dossiers Secrets* only drops hints as to their nature.

Anyone with a reader's card to the Bibliothèque Nationale can read the originals. There are also more accessible facsimile editions, published by French researcher Pierre Jarnac in the 1990s. They may not still be in print, but they were widely available in France.

*In* The Templar Revelation, *you say that the* Dossiers Secrets, *which Dan Brown uses as key to establishing links between several of the great secrets in* The Da

Vinci Code, *appear to be complete nonsense. Why?*

We say that because, in our view and at first glance, they *do* appear to be complete nonsense. Because so much of what's in them clashes with accepted history, it's tempting to just reject them as pure fantasy. But it's not as simple as that. While some of the information is demonstrably wrong and some deliberately misleading, some—unexpectedly—checks out.

Moreover, the *Dossiers* are mightily disappointing. They are *not*, as Dan Brown claims, romantic old parchments, but in fact, simply typewritten or cheaply typeset. It's hard to imagine great secrets being revealed on such shabby bits of paper.

*What is the direct connection between the Knights Templar and the Priory of Sion?*

The central paradox of the Priory of Sion is that there's no evidence of its existence before 1956, yet it claims that it's been around since the Middle Ages. In recent years, though, it's changed its story, claiming to have been founded in the eighteenth century.

The conclusion that we've come to since writing *The Templar Revelation* is that the Priory of Sion that declared itself to the world in 1956 *was* invented then, but as a front for a network of related secret societies and esoteric orders that *do* have a genuine pedigree. This front has allowed them to do certain things in a semipublic way without revealing who or what is really behind them.

In the *Dossiers Secrets*, the Priory of Sion claimed it was a brother organization to the Knights Templar, but there is no proof of such a connection. In any case, the Priory of Sion has since retracted the claim (if it was founded in the eighteenth century then obviously there was no connection!).

There was an Order of Our Lady of

Mount Sion that belonged to the abbey of the same name in Jerusalem that had some connection with the Templars, and it has claimed that the Priory of Sion is the continuation of that order, but unfortunately that's as far as it goes.

On the other hand, there's a close connection between the *modern* Priory of Sion and secret societies that claim descent from the medieval Templars. These neo-Templar groups can all be traced back to an eighteenth-century society called the Strict Templar Observance, which claimed—with some justification—to be the authentic heirs of the medieval Templars' secrets. And the organization led by Pierre Plantard [reputed grand master of the Priory of Sion in more recent times] acts as a front for these groups.

*What made the Templars so famous? What secret information are they supposed to be guarding?*

Historically, it is accepted that the Templars were unusually skilled in the fields of medicine, diplomacy, and the military arts—being the elite forces of their day. They acquired much of this knowledge on their travels, especially in the Middle East, and a good deal from their enemies, the Saracens, who were particularly renowned for their scientific knowledge. (One reason why the Saracens were so far ahead of the Europeans is that all scientific experimentation was banned by the church.)

There's no doubt the Templars also sought esoteric and spiritual knowledge—although you won't find much about that aspect of their *raison d'être* in standard history texts. The Templars were so secretive that nothing is known for certain about their hidden agendas: it's a matter for informed speculation. They've been linked to everything from the Ark of the Covenant and the Holy Grail to the Lost Gospels and the

Shroud of Turin. Nobody really knows for sure.

However, our research has indicated that the Templars were very much a society within a society: the mass of rank-and-file knights being no more or less than the good Christians they were supposed to be. But the founding knights and the continuing inner circle appeared to follow a different—and very heretical—agenda. It's known there was a big secret about Baphomet, the severed head that the Templar initiates were alleged to have worshipped. Was Baphomet really a head—a bearded, severed head, as some knights claimed? And if so, who or what could it represent?

## Who is Pierre Plantard?

Pierre Plantard (aka Pierre Plantard de Saint Clair) was grand master of the Priory of Sion until his death in 2000. He was their public face. With him, the Priory of Sion emerged into the public domain, mainly through the interviews he gave to Michael Baigent, Richard Leigh, and Henry Lincoln, authors of *Holy Blood, Holy Grail*—which led indirectly to Dan Brown's book. Who the grand master is now, or even if there is one, is a matter of conjecture.

It is important to stress that he

[Plantard] never said anything about the bloodline of Jesus and Mary Magdalene. That was Baigent, Leigh, and Lincoln's hypothesis. After their second book, *The Messianic Legacy*, came out [in the United Kingdom in 1986], Plantard explicitly repudiated that idea. [Dan Brown doesn't seem to be aware of this!]

*What is the Merovingian line and what is its connection to Jesus?*

The Merovingians were a dynasty of Frankish kings who reigned over parts of what are now northern France, Germany, and Belgium between the fifth and eighth centuries. They were usurped by the

Carolingians in collusion with the church.

The central contention of the *Dossiers Secrets* is that the Merovingian line did not die out, as history records, and that the Priory of Sion has protected its descendants throughout the ages to the present day. There's a suggestion that they are the legitimate kings of France, and that the aim of the Priory of Sion is to restore them to the French throne. This is absolute nonsensical rubbish. Even if the Merovingians survived, which is extremely doubtful, they would have no claim whatsoever to the throne—which no longer exists anyway in the Republic of France.

The central theory of *Holy Blood, Holy Grail* is the secret of the Merovingian bloodline and that it was descended from the children of Jesus and Mary Magdalene. This is the idea that particularly inspired *The Da Vinci Code*. We can't stress too much that this is *entirely* Baigent, Leigh, and Lincoln's hypothesis. It appears *nowhere* in the *Dossiers Secrets*, nor in any other Priory-related documents, and was explicitly repudiated by Pierre Plantard.

*What basis is there for thinking that the Holy Grail represents Jesus' bloodline through Mary Magdalene's womb?*

Baigent, Leigh, and Lincoln argue that the Holy Grail, the "vessel" that contained Jesus' blood and seed, is a coded reference to the womb in which Mary Magdalene carried his children. It's an intriguing but very debatable hypothesis, especially as the "vessel" idea of the Grail was not its original form. The first tales either didn't describe the mysterious Holy Grail as anything in particular or had it as a stone.

We absolutely do not agree with the Grail as Magdalene's womb theory. This was *explicitly* rejected by the Priory of Sion itself and is the central mistake of both *Holy Blood, Holy Grail* and, less seriously, *The Da Vinci Code*, which is, after all, fiction.

*Can you talk a bit about Leonardo and his link to a secret society?*

Historically, Leonardo is known to have been a heretic and to have been interested in esoteric ideas. The Priory of Sion claimed him as their ninth Grand Master—but whether this is literally true is impossible to say, although it is very unlikely. There's no contemporary document that makes such a link, but if we're talking secret society, there wouldn't be, would there?

But what is clear is that Leonardo incorporated symbolic elements into his works that fit with the themes in the *Dossiers Secrets*, establishing at least that both adhered to the same tradition.

For us, as we explain in our book *The Templar Revelation: Secret Guardians of the True Identity of Christ*, the key element is Leonardo's elevation of John the Baptist to the point that he seems superior to Jesus—even the "true Christ." Ironically, the chapter of our book that we called "The Secret Code of Leonardo da Vinci" (ring any bells?) was *not* about the alleged bloodline of Jesus, but actually about this "Johannite" heresy.

# Part III

Keeping
the Secrets
Secret

# 7 THE MYSTERY OF CODES

In the 1997 movie *Conspiracy Theory*, Mel Gibson plays the part of paranoid New York cabbie and conspiracy buff Jerry Fletcher, who clips articles from the *New York Times* which he believes contain coded information about the secret plans of NASA, the UN—and even Oliver Stone—to destroy America. Unfortunately, he accidentally turns out to be right with one of his conspiracy theories and, as with the boy who cried wolf, the wolves finally do come after him.

The movie illustrates how broadly conspiracy theories in general, and secret codes with hidden meanings in particular, have permeated the zeitgeist of modern society, American society especially. And to be sure, this widespread belief in conspiracy—the sense that "there's a covert force at work keeping things undercover and admitting only certain things to the public," to quote the real-life Mel Gibson and not his character—does have some foundation in reality.

After all, the government really did conspire in the Watergate and Iran-Contra scandals, and the church really did suppress evidence of widespread sexual abuse by its priests. The list of proven, true conspiracy tales in politics and in the courtroom uncovered by investigative journalism is frightening indeed.

As for secret codes, one does not need to believe, like Gibson's Jerry Fletcher or the schizophrenic John Nash in *A Beautiful Mind*, that *Life* magazine or the *New York Times* place hidden messages in their articles to recognize how ubiquitous and powerful secret codes have become in everyday affairs. Without them, business and finance would grind to a halt, our military and government could not function effectively or defend the nation against its enemies, and no citizen could shop online or get cash from an ATM. Secrecy of coded messages is now a daily front-page issue, whether as admonishments to keep one's Social Security or PIN number safe from prying eyes, or debates over who may copy the software code that defines digital music and images.

In every shocking event and mass tragedy, someone appears from outside the mainstream box to publicize a secret code and allege a conspiracy. September 11 was just such an example. On the one hand, thousands of people chatted across the Internet about secret signs and codes—everything from the meaning of the "911" date itself (a nearly universal American code for emergency), to the covers of rock albums and scenes from movies that, in our ultraviolent society, had depicted buildings being blown up. Otherwise seemingly intelligent people argued that the Bush administration knew 9/11 was going to happen, but, like FDR at Pearl Harbor, "wanted" it to happen to galvanize the country for war. Or that somehow 9/11 was a "Jewish conspiracy" designed to, designed to . . . well, no one who holds this view can actually articulate anything that makes enough sense to finish the sentence. But the motivations for entering into conspiracies are accepted by conspiracy theorists as irrational or unimportant. Thus, even with all the debate and discussion *The Da Vinci Code* has generated, almost no one has spent any time on how utterly irrational and illogical the motivations of "the Teacher" are for killing Saunière and the other sénéchaux, or how magnificently improbable a plot structure is that relies on an unholy alliance of the most dedicated Holy Grail hunters with those most opposed to allowing the "truth" of the Holy Grail to come out.

"At the end of an exhausting century," wrote *Newsweek* recently, "conspiracy is a comfortable way to make sense of a messy world. One-stop shopping for every explanation. Things don't just fall apart. Somebody *makes* them fall apart."

The public also wants heroes and heroines like Langdon and Neveu. Given all the crazy and conflicting information coming at us in our daily lives, we all wish we could be like these New Age superheroes in figuring out what's really happening and what it all means, and acting intelligently and heroically—mentally and physically—to solve problems and avert disaster. In this extended novel-length exercise in code-breaking, Robert and Sophie retrace the steps of Theseus, Odysseus, Moses, Job, Jesus, Frodo, and Harry Potter—and plenty of others from the world of the hero's journey in myth and archetype. They must crack the code before it is too late!

# Is God a Mathematician?

## AN INTERVIEW WITH BRENDAN MCKAY

Brendan McKay is a professor of computer science at the Australian National University. He achieved notoriety a few years ago by debunking the Bible code theory, most notably espoused by author Michael Drosnin, which claims that the Hebrew text of the Bible contains intentional coincidences of words or phrases (appearing as letters with equal spacing) that predict an impressive array of historical events from assassinations to earthquakes. McKay showed that by applying the same mathematical techniques used by promoters of *The Bible Code* to other books similar "amazing" predictions could be found (indeed, McKay noted that a mathematical "analysis" of *Moby Dick* even found a "prediction" of Michael Drosnin's death). As McKay noted at the time, "The results of our very extensive investigation is that all the alleged scientific evidence for the Bible codes is bunk."

In the 1990s, *The Bible Code* was as big a sensation as *The Da Vinci Code* is today. Although *The Bible Code* does not figure particularly in *The Da Vinci Code*, McKay's experience is a case study in the need for skeptical, critical thinking about hidden messages, symbols, and codes from the Biblical era.

*How did you first become interested in analyzing the Bible code?*

I'm interested in the study of pseudoscience as a discipline. And because I'm also a mathematician, it was natural for me to examine the Bible code theory as a mathematical example of pseudoscience, which I define as something that has a scientific appearance but, upon closer examination, can be shown to not be based on

scientific principles at all. What was
intriguing about the Bible code theory was
that some of the evidence for it was pro-
duced by qualified scientists, whose
work—at least superficially—looked very
convincing and scientifically solid.

*So what did your investigation reveal?*

Our finding is that the word patterns
and seeming predictions in the Bible are
there purely by random chance, and that
similar word patterns can be found in
every book.

It's also important to realize that over
the course of time the Bible has changed
a lot. Especially in the early days before

Christ, there were probably substantial changes. What's more, the Hebrew spelling practice in the Bible today—which Bible code proponents use as the basis for their supposed discovery of hidden messages—does not follow the practice in use at the time the Bible was supposedly written. It's been rewritten using updated spelling rules. Because of this, any messages that might have been encoded in the very original text have been wiped out. So the whole basis for the Bible code theory is flawed. From the scientific point of view, we can say that no evidence has been found for word patterns or hidden messages in the Bible except those you'd expect by chance. We demonstrated convincingly that you can do the same thing with almost any text.

But of course some people don't want to be convinced! So the debate never quite ends.

*Why do you think that is?*

It's much the same as any other type of occult belief, or for that matter things like conspiracy theories. There really isn't anything that you can do to stop people from believing in a good conspiracy theory. Because people really like believing things like that, somehow it satisfies some need they have.

*But what about the concept of sacred geometry or the divine proportion discussed in* The Da Vinci Code, *which describes the curious fact that the design proportions of man-made objects and even nature (the ratio of the length of your hand to your forearm) seem to follow a certain universal pattern defined as* Phi, *or 1.61804?*

I think there's a natural explanation for that. The universe operates according to a set of rules, and if the physicists are right, these rules are very few and quite simple. This almost automatically implies that some aspects of nature, including its design elements, are going to appear repeatedly in different guises. So the fact that something like the divine proportion appears in many different places—in the shape of coastlines, in leaves growing on plants and lots of other things—should not be too surprising. It does not indicate that there is some guiding hand behind it. It's just that the universe operates according to a fairly small set of rules.

*What about the Fibonacci sequence, which plays such a big role in Dan Brown's book?*

There are good reasons why the Fibonacci sequence occurs often in nature. It's a very mathematically simple sequence. Each number is the sum of the previous two. So each time you've got a system which evolves—a plant that's growing and more leaves are coming on it, and each new growth depends on the previous ones and the ones before that— you've got this sequence coming out. And the sequence also satisfies many other mathematical properties which could correspond to the way nature works.

*So is God a mathematician?*

Let's put it this way. According to modern science, the whole of nature operates according to mathematical principles. So anyone wishing to promote "divine" or mystical reasons for why things are the way they are is naturally going to try to cloak these in mathematical, pseudoscientific garb. Yes, they'll make God a mathematician.

# 8 LEONARDO AND HIS SECRETS

Leonardo da Vinci hovers over *The Da Vinci Code* from the first moment in the Louvre to the last moment in the Louvre. He is everywhere in Dan Brown's novel, looking over the shoulder of the plot with the Mona Lisa eyes that gaze out from the cover. Did he integrate a secret coded message into *The Last Supper*? And if he did, was it about Mary Magdalene and her marriage to Jesus? Was it more generally about women and sexuality? Was it a heretical in-joke? Was it a secret gay message? Or was it something even more obscure to us today about the relative importance of John the Evangelist and Jesus Christ?

Was Leonardo a secret devotee of the Templars and possibly a grand master of the Priory of Sion? Did he know anything about the Holy Grail beyond what other sophisticated Renaissance men knew? Did he believe the Holy Grail was not literally a chalice but the metaphorical or real womb of Mary Magdalene? Did he believe in the cult of the sacred feminine? (The aphorisms quoted above suggest he ascribed a feminine character to wisdom and knowledge, much as the Gnostics did.)

Why did he write in codes? There are many mysteries about Leonardo, and food for many more thrillers and flights of postmodern imagination to come long after *The Da Vinci Code* has become an answer to a trivia game question.

There are two basic schools of thought. The mainstream view, held by most Leonardo scholars and art historians, suggests that while there are innumerable mysteries and questions in the life and work of Leonardo, there is no evidence to support conclusions as far afield as the thinking that the John character in *The Last Supper* is really Mary Magdalene, or that Leonardo presided over the Priory of Sion, or that he was leaving coded messages behind in his art works to be interpreted in later eras.

The other view is certainly much more interesting, even if the evidence is thin. Their view offers fascinating answers to some of what the more-established experts can only point to as a long list of questions. This type of thinking about Leonardo may turn out to have little basis in fact. But it may have a lot to offer metaphorically and conceptually.

# Trying to Make Sense of Leonardo's "Faded Smudge"

## An Interview with Denise Budd

Denise Budd is a Columbia University Ph.D. whose doctoral dissertation on Leonardo da Vinci focused on a reinterpretation of the documentary evidence from the first half of his career.

*Is anything known about Leonardo that would suggest he was a member of the Priory of Sion or similar secret society?*

There's no real evidence at all that Leonardo da Vinci was a member of the Priory of Sion or any other secret organization. The documents that Dan Brown relied upon heavily were discovered, apparently, in the Bibliothèque Nationale in Paris in the 1960s, and they appear to be twentieth-century forgeries.

*Besides sometimes writing backwards, did Leonardo use codes or coding?*

There is evidence of codes in some of his writing; one example is the so-called Ligny memorandum, in which he interspersed names and places in scrambled letters. And he may have worked as a spy when he was a military engineer for Cesare Borgia. But the backwards writing is not a particularly difficult code to crack. That was a function of Leonardo's left-handedness.

*Leonardo is known for peppering his works with symbolism and, some say, heretical ideas, in his Virgin of the Rocks paintings, for example. Do you agree?*

No, I don't. The *Virgin of the Rocks* was a religious commission for the Confraternity of the Immaculate Conception for the church of San Francesco Grande in Milan—not for nuns, as Brown says. Leonardo da Vinci got the commission in 1483. There were some complex legal issues regarding it and its copy, including issues of payment for Leonardo and his associate, Ambrogio de Predis. One of the reasons that Dan Brown argues that the painting is heretical is because he misreads the work, confusing the figure of St. John the Baptist with Christ, and vice versa. The composition shows Mary—with her hand suspended over her son, creating a dominant axis—embracing Christ's cousin St. John, who kneels in reverence. The Baptist is the first to recognize Christ's divinity, which he does in the womb, so this composition falls completely within the norms of tradition.

With the added element of the angel

Uriel, Leonardo is actually combining two separate moments: this scene from Christ's infancy, with the scene when the Baptist visits the holy family on the flight into Egypt. Leonardo guides us through the composition by the play of hands, which relate the figures to one another. Presumably, the subject would have been worked out with the confraternity, and it would have played an important role in establishing the iconography, which likely refers to the issue of Mary's immaculate conception, which was not yet a matter of settled church doctrine. During the Renaissance, an artist was not generally given free rein on important commissions. There would have been specific guidelines. And presumably, Leonardo worked within that framework.

*What about Dan Brown's thesis about the* Last Supper*?*

There is no disembodied hand as Dan Brown suggests. The hand with the knife—which is the hand Dan Brown says "threatens Mary Magdalene"—that's Peter's hand. And Peter's not threatening Mary Magdalene nor trying to suppress the feminine side of the church. Peter is holding the knife, which is a premonition of the violent reaction he will have during the arrest of Christ, when he cuts off the ear of the Roman soldier. So that is a fairly standard iconographic tool.

Dan Brown uses the absence of a chalice as an introductory point to bring Mary Magdalene into the picture. Yet if you look at the picture, you'll see that Christ's hands are spread out on the table. His right hand is reaching toward a piece of bread, and his left hand is actually, quite clearly, reaching toward a cup of wine. And that's the hand that's pointed down. The institution of the Eucharist is clearly presented in the bread and the wine. Now it's not a chalice per se, like a chalice in your modern church practice, but there's a cup of wine. It's what you would expect to see at the Last Supper.

*And what about the idea that the painting depicts Mary Magdalene instead of John the Baptist?*

As far as the Magdalene, clearly there is no dispute. That figure is St. John the Evangelist. St. John is Christ's favorite and he is always shown by Christ's side. The major difference between Leonardo's *Last Supper* and earlier Florentine examples of the scene is that Leonardo put Judas among the disciples, not on the other side of the table. But the figure of John is always by Christ's side, he is always beardless and he's always beautiful. And in some instances, he is so innocent that while Christ is making the announcement that he will be betrayed, John actually sleeps. A perfect example of this "feminine" characterization of John is in Raphael's *Crucifixion* in the London National Gallery, painted around 1500.

A second point that must be mentioned is the atrocious state of the *Last Supper*, which makes it patently unreliable to examine for any reason other than basic composition, which, presumably, it retains. It was called a wreck only twenty years after its completion, while da Vinci was still alive, and has again and again been called barely visible. In the sixteenth century, Vasari called it a "faded smudge." It was restored in 1726, 1770; hung in a room that was used for a barracks for Napoleon's troops in 1799 and as a stable; damaged in a flood of 1800; a door was cut through the bottom of it; there was an attempt to remove it from the wall in 1821; it was restored in 1854–55, 1907–8, 1924, 1947–48, 1951–54, and all throughout the 1980s and 1990s. There is not enough of any of the faces

left to make any serious determinations.
Christ's face, for example, is a completely modern repainting.

# 9 TEMPLES OF SYMBOLS, CATHEDRALS OF CODES

## The Secret Language of Architectural Symbolism

Ever since the first artistic renderings of the human sense of the sacred were painted on cave walls, visual signs and symbols have been a key part of the experience and expression of the sacred, the divine, the ritualistic, and the religious.

In *The Da Vinci Code*, we spend a good amount of the twenty-four-hour experience inside churches—Saint-Sulpice, Temple Church, Westminster Abbey, Rosslyn Chapel . . . plus the Louvre Museum, arguably a veritable "church" in the opinion of Jacques Saunière. We also hear discussion of Notre Dame and Chartres, King Solomon's Temple in Jerusalem, and more. We also hear Robert Langdon, the symbologist, explain his theories about how the church architecture was designed to reflect the sacred feminine in many architectural and design aspects.

Egyptians, Greeks, and Romans all expressed their religious cosmology in how they designed and constructed their buildings. Certainly, Templars and Masons, master builders, expressed their belief systems in their architectural work.

In this chapter, we take a virtual tour of the main themes of *The Da Vinci Code* as expressed in architecture and visual symbols.

# The "Symbology" of *The Da Vinci Code*

## AN INTERVIEW WITH DIANE APOSTOLOS-CAPPADONA

Diane Apostolos-Cappadona discusses Brown's use of symbolism here. Although, as she points out below, she never heard the word *symbologist* (Robert Langdon's alleged field of expertise at Harvard) until she read Dan Brown's work, she is about as close as one can get to being a real-life professional symbologist.

*What is the importance of symbols in Christianity—and in religion in general?*

Symbols are a form of communication. However, this is a form of communication that is multileveled, or multilayered, in that there is no equal, one-for-one exchange. This is what makes them both fascinating and difficult, or confusing. Symbols operate on a variety of levels: they do such "simple things" as teach the ideas or the history of a faith or tradition, teach the stories of religious or societal traditions, teach religious doctrine, and explain how one is to gesture and posture and stand during liturgical services. They tell you about communicating with members of your community, and how to identify yourself within that community. There is the further understanding that symbols—and this principle is at work for all world religions, not specifically Christianity—are a way of communicating an embodied identity of knowledge and an embodied identity of who this community is. So symbolism and symbols are an integral part of the socialization process.

*Do the meanings of symbols tend to change over time?*

Yes, the meanings of symbols can change because of shifts in theology, doctrine, art styles, politics, and economic situations. For example, enormous changes in symbolism occurred during the Reformation, which was a complex umbrella of economic, political, and social transformations, as well as a religious revolution. This is the problem with symbols, and simultaneously the fascination; it's never as simple as a red light means stop and a green light means go.

*What symbols historically have been connected to Mary Magdalene?*

The most important one is the unguent jar, which relates to her being the anointer and connects her symbolically, if not metaphorically, to the other women anointers in the scripture, including the women who anointed the feet and the head of Jesus before the crucifixion. The female anointer who cared for—that is, washed, anointed, and dressed—the body of the deceased was a common role in Mediterranean cultures. These anointers were always women. It was taboo for men to wash and anoint the dead. Women were considered "unclean," so for them to wash and anoint the dead was not inappropriate; this may be a negative reading for women. However, you could relate this activity to a Jungian reading—that every man has three women in his life: his mother, his wife, and his daughter. Each woman initiates

him into a different part of his life—and
one of the functions of the daughter, ultimately, was to purify and anoint her par-
ents' bodies after death.

*What about the pentacle, which is used
as an important symbol in* The Da Vinci
Code?

The pentacle has five sides. The symbolic meaning is related to numbering,
numerology, and the significance of the
number five. In Christianity, five is the
number of the wounds of the crucified
Jesus (his two hands, his two feet, and his
pierced side). Five relates fundamentally
to the concept of "the human"—two

arms, two legs, and a head. Numbers have meanings. There are mystical numbers, normally odd numbers, and therefore indivisible. Seven, for example, is the number of fulfillment; there are seven days in the creation story. Three is a mystical number and so forth: three, five, and seven.

*Do you believe that the Holy Grail is a metaphor or a real object . . . or both?*

I believe that there has been—and always will be—a perpetual mythology about the Holy Grail. Further, there is a history of an understanding that the Grail was a true object, a physical object that could be touched, to which Christians would have had great devotion, and which for some reason disappeared. According to certain legends and popular traditions, the Grail disappears and then reappears in England, reputedly brought there by Joseph of Arimathea. The place in England where the Grail reappears is at the site we would identify as Camelot. Of course, the important principle is that the concept of the Grail is a metaphor for the spiritual quest. So to be honest, I suppose my answer is that it's both—both a metaphor and a real object.

There was a *Newsweek* article [*The Bible's Lost Stories*, 12/08/03] with a small sidebar, "Decoding *The Da Vinci*

Code," which included images of the
Last Supper and one of the Chalice of
the Abbé Suger now in the National
Gallery of Art in Washington, DC. The
alabaster part of that chalice was
believed to be the Holy Grail. Abbé
Suger had it encased in the gold and
bejeweled fashion that we have today,
and it was used at the first mass that he
celebrated at the Cathedral of Saint-
Denis in Paris, the first Gothic cathedral.
The building of this cathedral was, of
course, during the period of the
Crusades and the pilgrimages to the
Holy Land, when devout Christians
brought back as many major relics as

possible. The chalice has been tested—carbon-dated—and it's from the appropriate time period. However, I think of the Holy Grail more as a metaphor because the reality of history is that when Jesus of Nazareth and his followers had this meal together, they were not in a position, financially or otherwise, to have had this very elaborate tableware and other objects. If they were, would they have used a chalice? Or would they have used something that was more like a glass or a pitcher or a small urn?

The *San Graal* is a very important metaphor in nineteenth-century pre-Raphaelite painting and literature, with the revival of Dante and the Arthurian romances. The Grail is found in a variety of literary, musical, and dramatic productions, from the Ring Cycle by Wagner to *The Lord of the Rings*, in both book and movie formats. It is the same story over and over again: this quest for spiritual salvation. The tangible object being sought takes a variety of shapes, so that in these operas and the Tolkien works, it is a ring rather than a cup. In that way it's a metaphor.

*What about the idea put forth in* The Da Vinci Code *that the Holy Grail is actually Mary Magdalene?*

That's a very Jungian reading of Mary Magdalene—women as receivers and containers, women as vessels. But historically this is a connection that is older than Jung. You find this symbolism in classical mythologies. There are a variety of metaphors here. The mysterious connection in terms of sexual intercourse is the one that matters most. Women receive the male during sexual intercourse. They thereby conceive a child and hold that child in their sacred vessel, and then expel the child from their sacred vessel. I suppose one can make an argument for Mary Magdalene as the San Graal if one is a Jungian.

However, I have my own way of reading symbols, so for me it doesn't work. I think Mary Magdalene has sacramental importance, but that's not her primary importance. Who she is is a mystery, and that's what makes her great to write about. I think in the year 3000 people will argue just as much about who she is or who she was as they do right now. By that I don't mean arguing about a prostitute or a woman of means or a poor woman or a sexual woman; I mean how she is in Christianity perhaps the one mirror of all aspects of humanity. The one thing she isn't is a mother or a wife, as far as we know.

*What is the significance of Jesus appearing first to Mary Magdalene after the resurrection?*

Well, I don't think it was because they were lovers or, for that matter, possibly married as Dan Brown suggests. Rather, I think it was because she signified the witness—the one for whom seeing is enough to believe. This is as a parallel to Thomas, who had to touch the wounds and physically feel the body of Jesus—that is, the empirical evidence—before he would believe that Jesus had been resurrected. I think there are ways of reading scripture that argue for Jesus being very feminist. One way is that it is the women who continue to believe in him, who are faithful to him unto his death and provide the rituals of his death, his dying, his mourning, his burial; and it is the women who still come and who are not afraid. To me, the principle is that they represent that part of humanity that never loses faith, that never loses hope, the people for whom to see is enough to understand. To me it is empowering of women and of the feminine. Intuition is more important to me than reason. The Mary Magdalenes of this world trust their intuition, the Thomases do not.

*How accurate do you find Dan Brown's portrayal of Saint-Sulpice church in Paris—where a pivotal scene of the novel takes place—and its iconography?*

There is a reality that Christianity built churches, basilicas, and cathedrals on the sites of earlier religious buildings. There are churches throughout Rome, Athens, and France built on the sites of temples to Mithras, Athena, and other prior gods and goddesses. The most obvious is the church in Rome called Santa Maria Sopra Minerva—Mary over Minerva. However, the connection usually is more than architectural; that is,

Mary's church is built over the church of Minerva because there is a connection between Mary and Minerva as goddesses of wisdom.

For me, to propose that Saint-Sulpice is built over a temple or shrine to Isis makes no sense, because Isis connects to Mary the Mother more than she connects to Mary Magdalene. If parts of *The Da Vinci Code* were more about Mary the Mother, I might recognize the connection with Isis. For example, the Black Madonna cult relates Mary the Mother and Isis; so that the majority of the churches with black Madonnas were built on sites of earlier Isis shrines. So, yes, there is this whole tradition in Christianity.

*In* The Da Vinci Code, *Dan Brown's hero is a so-called symbologist. Is there such a thing, or such an academic discipline?*

The study of religious symbols is usually identified as iconography or religious art, not symbology. The first time I ever saw the word *symbology*, in fact, was in Dan Brown's *Angels & Demons*; I read his first book in this series of "Robert Langdon mysteries" first.

If such a term, symbology, were used as an academic or disciplinary title, it is part of what I do. I'm not a purebred academic in the sense that I research and study in an interdisciplinary or multidisciplinary fashion. I work with the arts, with art history, with cultural history, with the history of religion, with theology, with gender studies, and with world religions, so I don't have a pure academic discipline. However, I don't know of anybody who identifies him- or herself as a symbologist, and there is no formal academic study by that name that I know of. There may well be now because Brown's book has taken off.

# Part IV

## Conclusion

The spectacular publishing success of *The Da Vinci Code* has generated millions of satisfied readers, fans, and enthusiasts, on the one hand, and a wide variety of critics on the other.

Usually, when you talk about critical reactions to novels, you are talking about what literary critics and book reviewers say in the media that covers books. In the case of *The Da Vinci Code*, these critics were mostly very enthusiastic.

Calling it a "gleefully erudite suspense novel" and a "riddle-filled, code-breaking, exhilaratingly brainy thriller," Janet Maslin of the *New York Times* said she could sum up her reaction in one

word: " 'WOW.' Even if he had not con-
trived this entire story as a hunt for the
Lost Sacred Feminine essence, women in
particular would love Mr. Brown."

Patrick Anderson, writing in the
*Washington Post*, called it a "considerable achievement" to write "a theological
thriller that is both fascinating and fun."

Even many religious groups respond-
ed positively—if not to everything in the
book, then to the opportunity it afforded
them to introduce their own commentary
on the same subjects that Dan Brown
was addressing. Churches held retreats
and convened book groups; experts on
formerly esoteric issues (like the biogra-

phy of Mary Magdalene or the ideas contained within the Gnostic Gospels) were suddenly in great demand for church-sponsored lecture series.

On the website explorefaith.org John Tintera wrote, "Despite being somewhat simplistic, if not outright false, I think the religious content of *The Da Vinci Code* offers a timely wake up call to the Christian church. In doing so, it invites Christians to take a fresh look at our origins and our history, both the good and the bad, which is something we don't do often enough."

Soon, however, even as the reading public continued to lap up the adventures of Robert Langdon and Sophie Neveu, critics who don't usually write book reviews started to comment. Religious groups that took deep offense at what they believed was Dan Brown's desire to attack or defame Catholicism or Christianity began to be heard from. They wrote long commentaries on websites and in religious publications, responding to every idea in the book that they believed to be erroneous. In some cases, they were right about their facts, and Dan Brown was wrong—on matters like when the Dead Sea Scrolls were discovered or some of the details of what happened at the Council of Nicea. But in many ways, the religious critics were proving Dan Brown's point: they were so frightened by the novel's popularity and the possibility that it might supercede church dogma in winning hearts and minds to an alternative view of Christianity, they felt they had to engage in polemics with a writer of popular fiction.

The notion of Brown doing meticulous research also began to come under attack a few months after the publication of the book. Some saw *The Da Vinci Code* as highly derivative of books like *Holy Blood, Holy Grail* and

*The Templar Revelation*—books Brown cited by name in the text of *The Da Vinci Code* and credited on his website as important to his research. *Holy Blood, Holy Grail,* which has been circulating widely since its publication more than twenty years ago, is generally considered to be an occult stew of myth, legend, and outright hoax, mixed in with some very intriguing historical details.

Then another thriller writer came to the fore, Lewis Perdue, who had written an earlier book called *The Da Vinci Legacy* in 1983, and another called *Daughter of God.* These books featured

plot elements and characters that
Perdue asserted were remarkably close
to *The Da Vinci Code*. Among the similarities: a deep, dark secret from early
Christian history involving a Gnostic
female messiah named Sophia, dead art
curators, Swiss banks, Leonardo da
Vinci, Mary Magdalene, discussions of
goddess cults, and much more. A drama
may play out in the courts over these
similarities. But in the meantime, it
looks like another battle is looming in
Hollywood, where Ron Howard is
working on a film version of *The Da
Vinci Code* for Sony Pictures, while the
creator of *Survivor*, Mark Burnett, has

optioned the Perdue novels. We welcome our readers to join in the dialogue and post their own views on our website, www.secretsofthecode.com.

This book has been bound using hand-craft methods and Smyth-sewn to ensure durability.

Cover design by Leigh Taylor.

Book design by Jan Greenberg.

The text was excerpted from *Secrets of the Code: The Unauthorized Guide to the Mysteries Behind The Da Vinci Code*.

Abridged by Sarah O'Brien.

The text was set in Fenice and Times.

optioned the Perdue novels. We welcome our readers to join in the dialogue and post their own views on our website, www.secretsofthecode.com.

This book has been bound using hand-craft methods and Smyth-sewn to ensure durability.

Cover design by Leigh Taylor.

Book design by Jan Greenberg.

The text was excerpted from *Secrets of the Code: The Unauthorized Guide to the Mysteries Behind The Da Vinci Code*.

Abridged by Sarah O'Brien.

The text was set in Fenice and Times.

optioned the Perdue novels. We welcome our readers to join in the dialogue and post their own views on our website, www.secretsofthecode.com.

This book has been bound using handcraft methods and Smyth-sewn to ensure durability.

Cover design by Leigh Taylor.

Book design by Jan Greenberg.

The text was excerpted from *Secrets of the Code: The Unauthorized Guide to the Mysteries Behind The Da Vinci Code*.

Abridged by Sarah O'Brien.

The text was set in Fenice and Times.